FALLING LANDSCAPE

VAN K. BROCK
FLORIDA POETRY SERIES

ANHINGA PRESS

Falling Landscape

POEMS

Silvia Curbelo

VAN K. BROCK
FLORIDA POETRY SERIES
ANHINGA PRESS

Tallahassee, Florida 2015

Cover art: "Burb to Urb," by Thomas Barbèy
Author photo: Tom Errico
Cover design, book design, and production: Carol Lynne Knight
Type Styles: text set in Linotype Palatino
        and titles set in Trajan Pro Bold

Library of Congress Cataloging-in-Publication Data
Falling Landscape by Silvia Curbelo, First Edition
ISBN – 978-1-934695-42-5
Library of Congress Cataloging Card Number – 2014957235

Anhinga Press Inc. is dedicated wholly to the
publication and appreciation of fine poetry and other literary genres.

For personal orders, catalogs and information write to:
Anhinga Press
P.O. Box 3665
Tallahassee, Florida 32315
Website: www.anhinga.org
Email: info@anhinga.org

Published in the United States
by Anhinga Press
Tallahassee, Florida
First Edition, 2015

CONTENTS

IV

Acknowledgments

I'm grateful to the publications where many of these poems first appeared:

American Poetry Review: "Before the Long Silence," "Birthday Song," "Hearing the News," "Garden Party," "Learning to Play Coltrane," "Not This," "Jessica Gone," "Shine," "Headache," "The Law of Supply and Demand," "Snow is Falling on Our Good Intentions," "In the Locked Museum," "Painting Gala," "The Road Back."

Bloomsbury Review: "This Poem is Missing," "Between Language and Desire."

Caliban Online: "Notes on Courage," "The Sky Grew Dark, Then Darker," "I Would Dance with You Marie, But My Hands are on Fire," "I Dream the Lights are On in Our Old House," "Summerhouse," "Terra Firma," "Small Craft Warnings," "Hurricane Watch," "In the City of Drawers," "The Last Time I Saw Alice," "Ruby," "What Hope Is."

Crab Orchard Review: "The Visitors."

Gettysburg Review: "In the Land of Missed Chances," "Ambush."

Kestrel: "This Rain."

Luna: "Remembering the World As Children Once."

Maggie: "Losing Ground."

MiPOesias: "Falling Landscape," "Stain," "Traveling Light," "Sometimes the Sky."

Notre Dame Review: "Fifteen," "Barcarole," "El Patio de Mi Casa," "Joyride in Blue."

Tiferet: "Faith."

Some of these poems were reprinted in the following anthologies:

"Fall" in *Never Before: Poems About First Experiences* (Four Way Books). "Birthday Song" in *Birthday Poems: A Celebration* (Thunder's Mouth Press). "Learning to Play Coltrane," "Not This," "This Poem is Missing" and "In the Land of Missed Chances" in *Snakebird: Thirty*

Years of Anhinga Poets (Anhinga Press). "Garden Party" in *You Drive Me Crazy: Love Poems from Real Life* (Warner Books). "The Visitors" and "In the Locked Museum" in *Unexpected Harvest* (Kings Estate Press). "Between Language and Desire" in *The Aunt Lute Anthology of U.S. Women Writers,* Vol. 2 (Aunt Lute Press).

"Not This" also appears in *Sanctuary: Anna Tomczak Photographs* (Museum of Florida Art, 2008).

Finally, a number of these poems were collected in *Ambush,* winner of the 2004 Main Street Rag chapbook contest. My thanks to editor and publisher, M. Scott Douglass.

~

My deepest gratitude to Rhonda Nelson, Lisa Birnbaum, Hunt Hawkins, Don Morrill, Heather Sellers, Enid Shomer, Elaine Smith and Helen Wallace (my first Anhinga editor), who saw embarrassing early versions of many of these poems.

Thanks also to Francisco Aragón, Larry Smith, David Bonanno and Thomas Barbèy; to the Florida Division of Cultural Affairs, the Tampa/Hillsborough County Arts Council, the Writer's Voice and the Cintas Foundation for poetry fellowships; and to the Atlantic Center for the Arts for a safe haven.

Special thanks to W.S. Merwin and Campbell McGrath, also to Kristine and Jay Snodgrass, Rick Campbell, Don Caswell, Van Brock, Jeff Peters and the rest of the Anhinga family for 40+ years of great poetry, and especially to Lynne Knight for designing and editing this book, and for her vast patience.

A very personal thanks also to Pam Rubenstein and to my best peeps, Tom and Adrian Errico.

Falling Landscape

For Susan Hussey

For Gayl Christie

And in memory of my mother

Then they were gone
and the birds knew it.

Clouds drifted back
to some version of sky.

Absence became a feather.

I

Everywhere in the universe, it seemed
some great thing was gathering itself
— Stephen Dunn

EL PATIO DE MI CASA

On the last night we go as far as the edge
of the field. Then back. All around us
shadows of trees, the unattended rose garden.
The house hums with what we mean to say.

Time is a figure at the edge of a snapshot.
A sapling, a spigot, a darkness, a face.
We make walls from what the night
gives back, the stone of what we name

and name again. The black sky
is not a symbol. The child's bed is not a raft.
There is no narrative but this
thick gathering of clouds, this leaky roof,

as if the threat of rain could be anyone's story.
When I open my eyes the patio is empty,
rooted in sleep, equal parts mirror
and dream.

After the installation by Maria Brito

BIRTHDAY SONG

The day I was born I was
born screaming, weren't we all,
and who's to say there was no reason
to crawl headfirst into that vastness,
the great cathedral of what if.
I was alone and wanting and pissed off.
I felt the wind moving through it,
the sheer fact of desire entering
me like a long breath, obvious
as candlelight and cheap wine,
while happiness insinuated itself,
little flaws in the flesh.
Then one day it's ten minutes past the time
anything matters, and someone
is stepping closer through
the music, cutting slow circles
across the bright prairie
of dancing, moving among the loud
shirts and soft eyes of the newly lost.
And I can feel myself falling
like hard luck, like some poor excuse
for rain, or every notion that takes me
unawares, miles from everything,
knowing full well whatever fate
befalls me, gravity takes me
by the heart and sleeve.
Imagine a bed made for such
forced landings, the slow tumble
out of our own survival instincts, feathers
and grief, night falling where it will,
going down like barometric pressure,

while life plays like a blue movie
on somebody's dirty little bedroom wall.
And love still shines like the hall light
across those perfect ruins, a train
wreck of misspent youth and joy,
and doing it all over, with anyone,
while spread eagle loneliness
rubs its sore ankles on God's
infernal kitchen floor, black
square, white
square, the music careening over
everything broken, and rising,
and newly born.
Imagine someone moving closer
through that music, shrugging off
the wings, unbuttoning
the losses, then bending to touch
the tender corners of the cloth,
thinking how easily we could erase
the years gleaming on the table
with one eternal breath of praise
that puts out each small fire
as if it were a wish
and we were singing.

THE SKY GREW DARK, THEN DARKER

She could hear the wind's
coarse music like radio static in the trees.
She stepped outside to the smell
of grass and frying oil,
smell of lilacs, smell of ink.
And then the wind lay down
its load. It rained ribbons
and splinters. It rained salt.
Heavy drops fell onto her
closed eyes like pieces
of the answer, like an idea
pushed off a high ledge
then bouncing off her shoulders
like some cartoon loneliness
of rain. All around her people
scurried into cars and houses,
the day drifting on tiny,
complicated waves out to
some dim horizon where sky
meets all that isn't sky.
It rained like any mirror,
like a black and white movie
of the rain. It fell in great stripes.
It tumbled down like hair
landing brightly on her face
as only the rain can.

A Short History of Goodbye

The grass tells nothing.
The sky sits in its simple
cage of days. No sound
like the past blowing through.

Only the wind knows what's
at stake here, moving into
the scenery, running at the mouth.
Hush, say the daylilies

shaking their heads a bit.
Silence is its own music,
soft as dirt. No one notices
the orphan drift of clouds,

the wingtip scar of the horizon
balanced between nowhere
and this. *Hush*,
whisper the azaleas.

But nothing's as wordless
as a young girl standing on the lawn
waving her handkerchief.

I DREAM THE LIGHTS ARE ON
IN OUR OLD HOUSE

You come back as a wish
or a wave, daydream swimming
out of context, incidental
as loose grammar.
Like a bad haircut in a photograph
I'm good for a story, always
rooting through the weeds.
In the realm of the possible
I'm always arriving, constant
as a missed chance, a kind of
failure of the senses. *Touch here.*
And here. It's nothing
you can't wade through
in your Sunday suit.
I'm ancillary, converted,
still cashing in my chips.
I'm the heyday gone
to seed, subliminal in thigh-
high boots. In the soft
drive-in light of an old movie,
a kiss, a kiss, and later there's no one
to remember how it ends.
I'm aligned with the random,
poised for the overkill, butcher
knife in the cream pie, I'm moving
through some house-of-cards
moment while everything burns
or spills or tears apart,
shards of glass in the bath-
water, a kind of stripped-down
music in the key of what's left.

In the runaway sentence, syntax
scans the open road.
I'm a verb chasing a rumor.
It's the last day of spring and I have lost
my keys my hat my pickup sticks.
Words fail me, leave stubborn
handprints on the rumpled sheets
in a room where a light
burns and a voice whispers,
It's late. Open your eyes.
You'll never guess how long
we've been asleep.

Hurricane Watch

Sometime in the night a hole had opened up in the air of the room. It made a small wound at the center, but painless, a palpable lack. She thought it might be a kind of window or a door, but she wasn't certain. What wasn't there beckoned to what was left. Absence became a kind of weather to her. Wind darker than the road. The slowness of the hours was a mirror in which she saw herself. The clocks kept going. Tap water sitting around in an old glass. Somewhere miles away, thick clouds gathered and stalled. Trees moved the notion around like something broken. She thought she could make a story from the pieces. Something with windmills and numbers. Boredom. Rain.

HEARING THE NEWS

It is like fire.
It is a kind of burning.
Silence moves through it
like breath. It goes nowhere.
Where it begins it
ends, a notion surrounding
itself like a ring of flame.
It is nothing you have not heard before.
It is the essence of sound.
Imagine yourself there, not
there. It is the light falling
without you through trees
whose voicelessness
embodies the idea of you,
a burning thing among trees.
The way without you nothing
speaks and nothing
answers. Someone who is not
named, who is not there. Or
something that falls and is
not heard for many years,
but whose name is a constant,
a whisper of itself
among trees. The way
a child might imagine his own
death, distant and luminous
as a star. And burning.

SHINE

The day seemed strangely
out of context, black and white
as our hearts. We hated the smell
of sunlight in the alleys, the ruined
voices on TV. We couldn't read
between the lines. We craved
meaning and sleep, a hole
swallowing a hole.
Elsewhere there were trees,
there were sidewalks
and food. We had music and
cigarettes and cars, the ownership
of light and noise, loneliness, air.
As if a boy had smashed open
all the windows. As if
the ashen sky meant rain
and nothing more. At night
we saw dogs rooting in the shadows,
and men walking in the cold,
their hands drifting out of warm
pockets reaching for what? Solace?
A match? Imagine something
shines in the dark and something
moves towards that small
brightness. Haven't you
ever touched someone
in just that way?

SOMETHING WHISPERED YOUR NAME

In the first flare of sun along the water.
In the uppermost leaves of the dogwood.
In the dirt road and the chainlink.
In the theater of the rain
and the lake's shattered surface.
In the thin light of the history books.
In the bowl of dark fruit.
In bread, in salt, in memory.
In a dream's borrowed weather.
In the tender lies of morning
like a glass slipper
at the bottom of the well.
And once, without warning, the smallest
breeze on the back of my hands
passing through.

FALL

It was a wing, it was a kiss,
soft as a word, or as breath
in the middle of a word. It moved
through the air like smoke then fell
as quietly and deliberately
as any falling thing, a word,
a wing, a leaf, or sunlight
falling through leaves, heavier
than air, the way music
falls sometimes, or wind
after a storm has cleared.
But it was softer than that
really, like new snow falling
on the still-green grass by the side
of the road, or a certain kind of silence.
I thought there were clouds
in the distance. I thought
I saw an olive tree, or a birch, maybe.
I thought there was wind
and branches moving overhead
and the birds knew me.
It was a wing, a word, a blade, a kiss.
It was a song, it was a kind of singing
as if somewhere someone was singing
and I could hear the air moving
through it, that perfect rushing sound
like blood rushing over bone.
But it was more than breath, more than
music really, the vestige of some
elemental language suspended
in space, then falling the way a leaf
falls, or a voice, any voice.

I thought it called out to me.
I thought it said my name
in the pure reverence of light
and air, right where I stood,
the rain sinking its small
bright teeth into the earth.
But it wasn't rain, it was not
that kind of falling, not
rain, not a stone, never a stone
though I could feel the weight of it
the way a stone has weight
and texture, and language, and a voice.
And if I leaned my ear against
the trembling mouth of it
I could hear my own name softly
falling, a shining, falling thing
like a coin or a wish. It was
that real. It was in the air,
still falling.

Sometimes the Sky

To arrive at the facts without knowing.
To make strong coffee and watch the clouds
grow large and strange along the coast.
To feel the summer sky retreating,
taking its flower back.
To touch the page the cup the moment.
To get closer to it.
To remember rain falling on another house.
To step outside and find yourself
suddenly in a downpour, in a garden.
To kneel gently among the wet leaves.

THIS RAIN

Grass this green keeps its own secret.
It splits the world in two, the way love does.
This rain, and the terrible sweetness that comes after.
Beside the broken house of our childhood
wildflowers bloom, tiny embers
in an empty field. Whatever rain comes
is an afterthought, but it's always enough.
I can stand perfectly still in such a place
and hold that moment open. Not green
but the memory of green. The simple fact
of grass on a hillside. A secret becoming
larger with each telling. But nothing
should ever be that open or that green.
A flower turns away for a moment.
Something is falling inside the rain
and we can't hear it. And green
breaking the stem.

II

The Law of Supply and Demand

The pawn shops of the world are offering
their wares. Sunlight pours in

through the single window and it's
enough to know the sky goes on.

The street is ancient, it fends for itself.
Some are turned away hungry.

In a world of closed doors
something is unlatched and left

for broken. Whatever it takes,
there's a need and a cost.

The sky with its hundred false starts
where the nearly possible meets

the hopelessly undone,
the one promise it keeps.

Someone holds out the future
in his hands like a piece of bread.

Open this, he says.

GARDEN PARTY

The day makes its final appearance,
the sky rubbed out in places
with a blue so understated, it's nearly
a memory of blue. Forget the vase
arranged on the table, the tulips
are too vague. Even the white
tablecloth is an erasure.
Imagine the pale drone
of dinner conversation,
the politics of brie, cold soup.
The good china infects everything.
Even now the knife falters,
the wine glass can't be saved.
Think of the blank mirrors
of spoons, the fish
whose whiteness is a given.
Consider the ravenous napkin.

In the Land of Missed Chances

There was no news
in God's country. The sun
sank without warning.
Every ship sailed away.

No one sang for his supper
or looked for answers in the stars
or prayed for rain.
No one poured the last wine.
The dispossessed left nothing
in their wake.

There were no telephones
ringing, no music playing.
Nothing bloomed in the yard.
No one was lost or blamed
or left for dead.

There were no crimes to speak of.
The cops found no fresh signs
of struggle, no blood on
the sheets, no lipstick-smeared
cigarettes still smoldering in
ashtrays. No one gave up
the ghost or fell from grace.

Nobody rolled the dice
or held the winning card.
The last of our luck ran out,
swallowed the key
and closed the book.
We didn't have a prayer.

RUBY

Every storm is Jesus
chasing spirits, twister blowing
through the clothesline of the dead.
There's a sure thing in the high wind,
old as some stick in the ground.
Time makes an hourglass
out of anything.
Forget thunder, forget
the reckless past.
Keep your hymns short
and your fuse shorter.
Tell your children there's
no free ride to the reckoning,
no blaze-of-glory color
to paint this wicked world.
Blue is some skinny dog
lapping brown water
on the side of the road.
Green is his cup of sorrow.
Red is for knowing who's blind.

SMALL CRAFT WARNINGS

When the day slips out of context.
When wind shifts in its tracks
and the clouds fold in on themselves.

When birds let go of their shadows.
When the glass is half full
and wine spills on a lace sleeve.

When weeds unlock a hidden garden.
When the clouds part and the smoke clears
and the road stretches to its vanishing point

in the pure geometry of a dream
like a story that begins in a house by the sea
and ends anywhere the sky goes.

TRAVELING LIGHT

Certain roads need no metaphors.

Between the black rocks and the sea, the brave day.

Margins are essential to every situation.

What I mean to say is that, marginally, life goes on.

A dog works for its bone, hating the idea.

The usual notion of someone to lie down beside.

The real is like a train leaving an enormous station.

Nothing beyond it but some tracks and the promise of good
weather.

A sound like many drawers sliding shut.

The way, in the distance, a bird makes a world out of the air.

Tired of the story.

Already thinking of someplace else.

NOTES ON COURAGE

Take wing. Take charge.
Take cover. Take the last train
back to the start. There are no riddles
to be solved. There is no more dancing
around the facts. Take heart,
take the loss. Take this moment.

Let's forget everything we know.
Let's cut away the loose ends
to the meat of the story.

Take back night's 40 winks,
its burning fence, its brown sleep.
Forget faith. Forget universal truths.
Rake the leaves. Torch the letters.
Take back the fiery kiss,
the permanent deal.

Lose your grip. Lose your heart.
Lie down in ruins. Follow the last surviving army
through the proverbial burning forest.

Take back the night sky, the full complement
of stars. Forget heartbreak.
Forget the reckless past, your sweet
impaled youth, apple lost
in a wilderness of arrows,
the sleeping clothes of the new.

Take the high road. Be gone.
Take all the weather with you.
If memory taps you on
the shoulder, take it all back.

Have the last word. Take a stand.
Take no prisoners.

Let's make it count. Let's start over.
Let's take comfort in knowing
there's a way back.

THIS POEM IS MISSING

The difference between a mountain
and an abyss is a question of perspective.

Every mirror is an island
we're rowing toward.

Look how this moment disappears behind a cloud.
I never said the world was substantial.

Even as it conceals it,
the glove imitates the hand.

The air around a flower
is also the flower.

A basket of roses speaks for itself.
Silence is another thing altogether.

If nothing falls in the forest
does it matter who isn't there to listen?

Sorrows outnumber trees.
A man drinks to his orphaned heart

and swallows the voice
of what is missing.

The poem inside the mirror is
no dream, but tell me,

who will console the dreamer?

SWIMMING TOWARD SLEEP

Awake is an island, blue
stone under the rumpled bed,
refrigerator light that won't go out.
Awake is a hothouse mirror, knife
glint in the roses, piano wire
stretched across a great divide.
Paper cut, wrong answer,
torn scab someone keeps scratching
with a kitchen match.
Aquatic, you set your sights
downstream, where sleepers ride
the sweet current clutching
the hide of some dream animal,
while you stand on the banks
of your lost causes, dark oar
testing the water,
inconsolable, grounded.

WEATHER PATTERNS

Sunlight forgives everything
it touches, erasing every stone
in its path. Salt on its palm,
it cracks open the shell of any
story, thick as kindness moving
through the grass. But rain
leaves no blade unturned.
It lays a stubborn hand
on the horizon, pushing down.
Into the ground. Into the dark
earth. Where small things bloom.

III

Only the past is true.
— James Galvin

WHAT HOPE IS

Think of the weight of tenderness
or faith. What is willed, what

is opened. The way someone
whispers someone's name

into a glass, then empties it,
swallowing that small word.

SNOW IS FALLING ON OUR GOOD INTENTIONS

Someone has left the window open
and a cold wind parts the
quiet air as delicately as hands
lifting a veil, turning
the darkness over, a few late
stars still left in the sky.
In some rooms the mirror
never sleeps. Snowflakes
live behind glass for days,
holding themselves up
through any weather.
On nights like these any prayer
is an island. The way it keeps
everything hopeful and
surrounded. The voice
blooms at the corners
of the mouth and begins
its version of an answer, faith
tugging at the seams of
the familiar, bold as any
flower, no braver than this
kiss.

LEARNING TO PLAY COLTRANE

She thought it was green, not
the emerald green of Indian summer
but a green like a darkening plain,
or the shadow rivers cast.
She thought it was light, a glint
or a warning, the shine
at the papery edge
of storm clouds. The way
a voice rising and falling becomes
a premonition, a dampness
at the back of her neck. Or maybe
it was more of an imprint,
a memory of sound, some afternoon
after the circus has left town
and all that remains is a field
strewn with garbage, a music
of pasted stars and ruin.
And she thought of a color
like that, mud-green, the green
of a small sadness, shapeless
as the wind itself. And for a moment
she owned everything inside it,
the light, the field, the wind.

— for Adrian

STAIN

The young doctor, younger than imaginable,
said you could bleed for a week, maybe longer.
Maybe there's wisdom in that. A bandage
blooming like a word, casting a stain
onto the blank walls of a story, maybe this one.
Maybe young is not the point. Whistle-clean,
waiting for anything. A kind of ticking in the blood.
The way a woman might wait up all night,
but no phone call. Red of her hope,
hands stirring the pot. Red of what takes hold,
finally, by morning. Soup bone tossed into the weeds.
Her book of wind cracked open. Maybe young
is not so simple. Heart stirring in some other garden
and a voice moving through all that music.
Not thinking about the repercussions.
Not giving a damn how the song goes.
Just walking through deep grass with your hands open.
Stepping out of the shadows without warning.
Small red flower pinned to your lapel.

DRINKING AT THE BAR
THE UPS MAN GIVES YOU IDEAS

Send lies
Send bus fare

Send the hair you've plucked from his brush—
he'll need it more than you

Send neckties, spoons, pencil shavings

Send all your childhood scars and potions
The relics from Catholic school

Biographies of martyred saints
and jars of fresh honey blessed by monks

Send a list of every place you lost your heart
or your bearings

The twenty-seven arrows of bad love
and counting

Shot glasses, moth balls
pocket watch with the hands ripped out

and the smashed wings of a sparrow

Send it all C.O.D.
No questions asked

Return receipt requested

FIFTEEN

In the branches of sleep,
in the room's perfect hive,

incomprehension catches fire.
His youth like a strange song

deep in his throat. From her mother's
abandoned picture books

gardenias hum, their pale
green scent empty as a door.

Knowing is not responsibility.
A feeling not unlike ash under her tongue.

Through a forest of wings
the television answers.

Everywhere the trees burn.
Who can understand such longing?

Rubble of words and leaves.
A boy fumbles through dark pockets.

A girl lights a cigarette.
And the match blows.

BARCAROLE

In dreams the music never
fails us. It spins and swirls,

a woman's glittery skirt,
and our unhappy childhoods

rise into sudden air
like so many small birds.

Beneath the drift and pull of memory
a boy climbs a tree.

Hand over fist, the truth follows.
Something rattles the shadows.

A ripple, a small breeze
lifting the palest hair.

The way a stranger might touch
a careful finger to his lips

just as the boy lets go of the branch.

SUMMERHOUSE

I never said those things
about your mother. It wasn't me

with my eyes nailed to the wall,
inhabiting the air like a vase

of cut flowers, or pacing
the floor of that house

where sorrow slept. It wasn't
a rumor. It wasn't in spring

when azaleas overran the driveway.
No one believed what happened

didn't happen. But I can tell you,
the roses were on fire.

And didn't it rain. Didn't we
stand in the flowering light

of that storm while daylight
served up its version of the facts

like pages from a book of miracles
or a table set for two.

I couldn't eat a thing.

IN THE LOCKED MUSEUM

House of sleep, house of a long winter,
what moves through these rooms
is the past, windblown
as any field and just as green.
House of light, of dust
trembling in cupboards, lifted
as a child's voice is lifted,
the plain syllables of regret
like piano notes locked
in a tin box for years.
House of secrets, whisper
of shards and leaves, of wind
that stirs the ancient garden
and blows the old lilacs
to ruins, their deep,
clear scent drifting across
the wet stones of the courtyard
where the young Schubert
is peeling an orange in the rain
and feels the juice soak through his shirt.

Remembering the World As Children Once

1

The dream doesn't reach all
the senses. The hand, for instance,
encircling a cool glass closes
around air. The dream house slumps
into vagueness, another kind
of sleep where morning opens
to a scent both distant and familiar.
Freud would say this is not memory.

2

The eyes cannot see the whole
picture. They remember things
differently. In their version
of the story music drifts
through the open windows
and the white curtains fan out
as if the room itself had
wings, could rise beyond the reach
of the familiar, the vanishing
architecture of *I want, I need.*
Every note a small city in the trees.

3

Beyond the window, past the leaves,
the simple sky continues, a narrative
the river takes for granted.
In memory we are no more
than children, or the voices
of children. What we say to one another
does not change. Bridge to bridge
the river always answers, a hurt
like the beginning of the world.

4

In a dream a child disappearing
into himself could enter
any story. Now you see him, now
you see him less clearly.
Coins of light filter down
through the trees.

5

Sleep cuts loose its ancient raft
and the eyes drift through it.
In the dream's natural progression
a child becomes a wishing well.
His closed mouth is a promise
the way a cloud in any story
about rain is rain. A rustling
of wings up in the leaves
is the blueprint of an absence,
daylight slipped under the door
like a last letter carrying the news.

Terra Firma

How it came to you once across
that sudden prairie, great surge
of sky, how it raced through you
suddenly here, suddenly gone
cloudburst, spill, that otherness
of distances, both want and flood
a rushing toward and rushing
against, breath and nerve
and collarbone, how it filled the air
whirlwind, mouth kiss, all that
narrowness opening up at once and
at once in a flurry of yes and flash
and sky, how the air broke
around you, how you stood your ground

SMOKES

Empty bottle on the windowsill. Nothing walks into view.
Across the street they've finally sold the Flying Cloud Motel
and Trailer Park and in its place looms another used car lot.

Suppose the bottle is half full, maybe bourbon.

I long to exit in a swirl of perfume.

Something enters my mouth, smoke from your cigarette,
an insect, my old name. Whatever it is makes
my throat tighten and release, and it's like stepping

an inch outside myself and breathing that strange air.
And memory dragging its little dog
and chain.

~

You were working in that Japanese bar down by the water.
Nothing but time because your boyfriend was in jail.

I came for the free drinks and the cool suburban light.

Your pretty brother handing out hot washcloths
in his too-bright shirts. The tourists and the sunsets.
Grit of warm sand between our teeth.

That was the year nobody slept. Dead Elvis on every car radio.

You slap drinks down without a smile
for big tips and no small talk.

Polyester kimono the color of new money.

Long shifts blurring into dawn.

The future is a line drawn across the dirt
and you cross it.

~

Every sunrise the perfect slideshow for your Italian
movie soundtrack.

Over your left shoulder that house. Spanish mission
gone to seed. Crushed velvet drapes at war
with daylight. The heavy artillery of cheap wine.
Mi casa es su casa.

Statuary in the front yard. The history of the Italian
Renaissance rendered in plaster-of-Paris and four strings
of Christmas lights.

The little bridge leading to every bad road your mother
warned us about.

Reading by swimming pool light, making water angels
in the deep end. Mottled sky of the screen door closing.

Ashtrays, apples, matchbooks, beer.
Crushed box of Merits at the bottom of your purse
and the smell of rain coming.

~

I don't know what parallax means exactly, but it must have
something to do with passage and return,

the heart still in the crosshairs.

The way some nights everything shifts just slightly and it's
like walking into a room some part of you once inhabited
that's gone, that carries your absence like a blueprint.

Remembering is a tenuous bridge back to that center.

From where I'm standing the bottle is half full.

A long cigarette is burning between your fingers
even now.

HEADACHE

I woke up in a strange place,
in a dream, in a nest of fireflies.
When I opened my eyes I was
in a garden splintered by sunlight,
red roses seeped through the pale
leaves and the grass hummed.
The tepid air filled my lungs
like music, something French
and sentimental. I wanted
to sing, and why not?
I thought I was still dreaming.
I wanted a cigarette, a bath,
a glass of milk.
There was a small city behind my eyes
with roads and trees and newspapers.
I could feel it clanking to life,
its dogs and cars and crusty loaves
of bread, its bicycles and
postage stamps, its hundred
excuses for living, black coffee, rain.
It was a Monday or a Thursday,
I'm sure of it, and daylight
lay across my eyes like a net
of blunt knives. I wanted to wash
the bright taste of sunlight
from my tongue, I wanted sleep,
I wanted an answer.
My life was a dull museum,
a magazine, an accident
of fashion, rakish and foolish
as a white silk scarf. I was in a garden,
I could hear bells tolling across
fields, across churchyards and

parking lots. I could hear couples
breathing in their cars, old men
on park benches, I could hear lilacs
blooming, radios, bees.
I wanted to bask in the harsh light
of possibility. I wanted to lie on a red velvet
couch under a skylight, to lose all sense
of proportion and live without pity or
blame, without a trace of irony.
I wanted wind and all its
consequences, leaves
in my hair, and honey, not sugar,
for my tea. I wanted absolution,
I wanted an aspirin.
I wanted to nail all the windows open,
to memorize each searing blade
of light, each speeding train
between the eyes, each brooding
way the body answers, the soft and
crooked places where the bones meet and sing.

BETWEEN LANGUAGE AND DESIRE

Imagine the sound of words
landing on the page, not footsteps

along the road but the road itself,
not a voice but a hunger.

I want to live by word of mouth,
as if what I'm about to say

could become a wall around us,
not stone but the idea

of stone, the bricks
of what sustains us.

These hands are not a harvest.
There is no honest metaphor for bread.

THE VISITORS

They stand without pity or shame
like tourists on the bridge to your next
great sadness. They have been walking
in bad shoes. They want a cold beer.

They've come with their one small
suitcase, and night's implausible
laundry list. It's late.
They're tired of being poor.

All day the wind fails them, so does
the sky unloosening its sullen
Esperanto. They know the hard
currency of coffee and cheap cigarettes,

the accidental prayer of rain
on a car roof. Priests of indecision
and poor judgment, they reach into
the ancient dark to pull a coin out of thin air.

Call it a gift, a simple benediction,
as they move tenderly through the door
of your best life, whispering
Take it, it's yours. Write this down.

— for Ann

IV

AMBUSH

The room. The white piano.
The stars gone slack.
The unmistakable rising up
to meet her. In heels and
a dark suit. A green light. A wing.
An accomplice. Silence and
more. Not silence. The mandolin still
trembling, still holding its moan.
Scar of light on the page. The blade
of an old story. The hand, the voice,
the deep pocket. Whatever stars are left.
The map, the spit and polish.
The sky like a great pond.
The drift. The notion.
The wine with its warm hide.
The lavish hand grenade. The stars and more.
The cloud, its soft harness.
The well. The wound. The warning.

NOT THIS

It's not the way the light haunts
that particular landscape, or how clouds

in the distance imitate the world at rest.
The way the curtains hold the late

afternoon is not an issue. It's not
the lilies abandoned on the table,

or the dog lying beside her, or the wine.
It's not the weight of memory

on his eyelids. It's not the empty cup
he carries walking home in the dark

through fields brimming with sleep,
or the precarious raft of her

mouth on his, or her hands
in the evenings

putting cold cream where her youth had been.

Winter Morning, 1968

Mother's cane rings out of the past,
south of the weather, clink
of metal touching earth, the one kiss
I can live a whole life to forget.

When morning opens the shutters,
bare trees shore up the white rim
of the sky — 6 a.m. with its vague
scent of anywhere.

Her cane wants to be a bird.
Behind us, the frozen lake is a bridge
of photographs, the tin cups of her eyes
filling with sailboats, seagulls, waves.

This is a story like a suitcase filled
with snow. But she has never seen snow,
never cupped her hands around
that strange flower frozen in space.

And what is childhood but wishes
and feathers, the little balcony
made of sugar and salt, history
without interpretation. Ashes fall

from a place where nothing burns.
I wake to violets in my mouth,
the taste of Sunday morning,
smell of bread and sunlight in her hair.

I Would Dance with You, Marie, but My Hands are On Fire

— Bob Dylan

I would carry this weight on my tongue.

I would lay it down like dirt.

I would tend the black fruit.

I would torch the four corners of sleep.

I would cut down the stars from their dark hive.

I would rise from your dreams like a soldier.

I would soften the blows with these wings.

JOYRIDE IN BLUE

What is lost, what is broken,
the sweet slide of two worlds
colliding into night. Call it
a journey, a geography,
tangle of wires and TV light,
the insomnia glow of boredom
that has you reaching for the car keys
one hundred miles from morning, bone-
tired white flag of 6 a.m.,
as you slip behind the wheel
with the radio wide open.
And the street like a face in every mirror,
pulling you out from that starting place
where home and motion intertwine,
steam on the shaving mirror, gold script
on the blue towel, *His*. Not his.
But this is not the stone you carry,
work boots and wanderlust, the clatter
and hum of being alive, full-ride nightscape
splashed across your windshield like the back hand
of forgiveness, a kind of loose rain in the weeds
and empty lots of L.A., past the sinewy
figures of love, ghost deals gone sour
and a song in every shot glass.
Let's call it the blues, barkeeps
and cabbies cashing in their fares
to head home before the day breaks open
with its backslide of regret.
But not yet, not this moment,
windows rolled down to whatever
wind flies in, slow grind of salt
and blue neon, past lit up
tenement windows, museums

of rust and moving on. And desire
like an afterthought, all flash
and blur, the last-ditch starlight
of ten thousand cigarettes going in the dark.

After Carlos Almaraz's "Night Magic (Blue Jester)"

LOSING GROUND

A lie crawls into spaces
the wind opens, loses

its nerve at the scene of
the crime, settling somewhere

between your collarbone
and your best clean shirt.

A lie forgets your name,
denies your latest

indiscretion, invoking
every saint in the book,

pokes a beer-soaked finger
into the wound and stirs.

It empties your wallet
at the track, stalls out

at the corner of bad luck
and consequence, smokes

the last pack of Marlboros
you keep hidden in the shed.

A dark horse, a mirage,
it presses its face to every

keyhole, unfurls its gin-and-tonic
headache behind your good eye,

quiet as a mirror,
looking you dead on.

In the City of Drawers

There was a different life
inside this life. She knew it
and kept still. She felt it as

a kind of humming in
her chest, the sound lifting
her from harm. Music

like a window soaked
with light. It's clear,
a woman hides things

from view. People
move through the streets
without knowing. Accepting

the pale dress over her
recklessness. Refusing
the sweet pull of rage

or need. Her body unlocking
its brave secrets, an apple
shining in a tree. That's

how he found her. Her
scent rising from many
drawers. What Freud said

about desire. A man knows
his place among objects.
But the skin sings and sings.

PAINTING GALA

Gala in childhood. In rain.
In white garments. On a train
with a book and a suitcase.
Gala with swans, untouched
by sadness, feathers
tumbling from her mouth.
Without shoes. With a glass
of warm milk, sitting
crosslegged in the garden chair.

Gala in a taxi. In sleep.
In love with silence, her good
friend, her confidante,
and behind her left shoulder
the road. A madonna,
a bird, a many-
ringed thing like a tree
trunk. Windblown.

Sullen as a starfish.
Marooned, a beached
thing, moonlight spreading
the great satin sheet of her dreams.
Her pillow licked by flames.
The nightgown burning. Torn loose.
Rising like smoke, like Gala

in her suit of lights. So many
stars in her arms, so many
dead leaves. Gala with stormclouds.

In freefall. With pearls in her lap
and blood money in her fist,
a sudden loneliness

in the folds of her green dress.
So many untold distances
unfolding from her
whispering fingers. Awash
in sunlight. Lounging poolside
with a paper umbrella in her drink.
Swallowing every wish.

THE LAST TIME I SAW ALICE

She was wearing silk pajamas.
She was counting rabbits in her sleep,
sliding the heavy book onto the shelf.
She was losing the light, making
shadow puppets with her hands —
Look I'm a frog I'm a dancer
I'm an alligator up a tree.
She was falling in love again,
running out into the street
amid traffic and birds.
She was singing that stupid song
about ashes and roses, and nailing
all the feathers down.
She was digging her way
out of the sand, drinking
rum and cussing at the scenery,
like a pirate in that children's book
where the hero chews the treasure
map and swallows
while the girl swims to safety
in her slip. And there's blood
on his white shirt. And there's
the shoreline with its palm trees waving,
and that spot near the rocks where
the wind erased her yellow hair,
her voice, the blade between her teeth,
till she's the outline of a thought in your head,
the blank in this story,
a promise standing in the weeds,
the silver shovel in her hand.

JESSICA GONE

Silence lifting the latch,
unbuttoning the dress, fingering
scarves that wind as
the road winds.
The cut roses understand
there's safety in numbers.
Someone ladles soup
into a bowl. Someone
touches the black hair,
the single gardenia
helpless as a love letter,
prayer, snow on the ground.

FAITH

Sunday morning empty
as two stones, tethered
to nothing
Empty as a room
or a face undone
by memory
like a song the wind
carries
then lets go
Empty as letting go

Emptiness of wind
across the valley
and the rain that falls without
astonishment
on the bare grass
Emptiness of grass, then
and of roads going back
to the start—
a map, a bridge, a canvas, a shore

or waves released
against that shore
Or a landscape touched
by nothing
anchored to nothing
Not a harbor
but a story, a bandage, a voice

THE ROAD BACK

All she asked for was a clean
shirt and quiet and a safe place to land
All she asked for was a window
overlooking a stream, some
railroad tracks, or a road
a stone's throw from anywhere
All she wanted was a good book
like an island and a steaming
bowl of rice, white clouds
in the alley, white
stone lifted from her mouth
A song, a boat, a way of going
All she wanted was a field,
and snowmelt, and a river,
and the wisdom of sparrows
in the yard, their brief
precarious histories like a promise
no one expects to keep
And all she wanted was a clean slate
of sky like a freshly washed
handkerchief, a brightness
she could taste on her tongue,
and soft dirt, and a hillside,
and hands to let go

FALLING LANDSCAPE

Not this chair, not this room.
Not this questioning glance
or the birds outside her window,
or the wind rising through what comes next.
Not her name, her true calling,
the way the trees moving in unison
remember every voice.
Not this kiss, this connection,
hands filled with what spills over
from each cup. Not this bridge.
Not this answering place, or the blue black
of secrets under her tongue
when we stood at the mouth of what is broken
and trembles in each thing. And what
did we find there? What sound shattered
the brick and mortar of that moment?
And what of forgiveness, its plates
and bones? Not this room,
not this page. Not this emergency.
Not the grass opening like any mirror.
Not these trees. Not some leveling wind.

Before the Long Silence

Some words open dark wings
inside us. They carry us off
in the telling, the air going on
beyond language, beyond breath.

It's the small moments
that change everything.
On the last night my father
woke from a long, restless sleep
and pointed to a corner
of the room. *A bird,* he said.

NOTES

"Falling Landscape" is the title of a painting by William Pachner. While the poem of the same title on pg. 74 is not based on that painting, certain elements of this book were influenced by Mr. Pachner's work.

Pg. 5. "El Patio de Mi Casa" is the title of an installation by Cuban artist Maria Brito. This poem was written as part of "Pintura: Palabra, a project in ekphrasis," which pairs Latino poets with the work of artists featured in the Smithsonian American Art Museum's touring exhibition "Our America: Latino Presence in Visual Art." Pintura: Palabra is an initiative of Letras Latinas, the literary program of the University of Notre Dame's Institute for Latino Studies. I'm grateful to Francisco Aragón, director of Letras Latinas, and Emma Trelles, our workshop facilitator, for the opportunity to be part of this project.

Pg. 26. "Ruby" is based on the work of outsider artist Ruby Williams.

Pgs. 38, 43 and 60. "Snow is Falling on our Good Intentions," "Barcarole" and "Not This" are based on works by artist/photographer Anna Tomczak.

Pg. 39. "Learning to Play Coltrane" is for Adrian Errico.

Pg. 41. "Drinking at the Bar the UPS Man Gives You Ideas" borrows its last line from "Easter Parade," a poem by Rhonda J. Nelson.

Pg. 50. "Smokes" is for Linda Grimm.

Pgs. 56 and 72. "The Visitors" and "Faith" are loosely based on a series of email conversations with novelist Ann Darby about the writing process.

Pg. 62. The title "I Would Dance with You, Marie, But My Hands are on Fire" is from a line attributed in conversation to Bob Dylan in the Martin Scorsese documentary, *No Direction Home*.

Pg. 63. "Joyride in Blue" is based on the painting "Night Magic (Blue Jester)" by Carlos Almaraz. This poem was written as part of the Pintura: Palabra project referenced earlier. (See notes for pg. 5 on previous page.)

Pgs. 67 and 68. "In the City of Drawers" and "Painting Gala" are inspired by the work of Salvador Dalí.

Pg. 70. "The Last Time I Saw Alice" is for Gayl Christie.

Pg. 71. "Jessica Gone" is for Jane Nobel Maxwell and in memory of her daughter.

Pgs. 73 and 74. "The Road Back" and "Falling Landscape" are for my mother.

ABOUT THE AUTHOR

Silvia Curbelo was born in Matanzas, Cuba, and emigrated to the U.S. with her family as a child. She is the author of three other poetry collections, *The Secret History of Water* (Anhinga Press), *The Geography of Leaving* (Silverfish Review Press), and *Ambush* (Main Street Rag Publishers).

She has received poetry fellowships from the National Endowment for the Arts, the Florida Division of Cultural Affairs, the Cintas Foundation and the Writer's Voice, as well as the Jessica Noble Maxwell Memorial Poetry Prize from *American Poetry Review*.